IT'S NOT TURKEY FOR
IT'S TURKEY THE COUNTRY!

GEOGRAPHY EDUCATION FOR KIDS

CHILDREN'S EXPLORE THE WORLD BOOKS

BABY PROFESSOR
EDUCATION KIDS

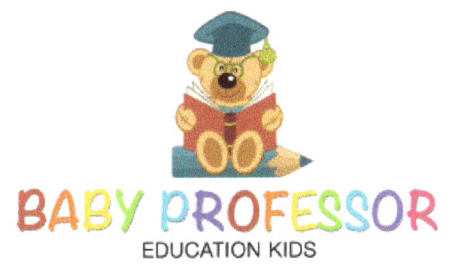

Speedy Publishing LLC
40 E. Main St. #1156
Newark, DE 19711
www.speedypublishing.com
Copyright 2017

All Rights reserved. No part of this book may be reproduced or used in any way or form or by any means whether electronic or mechanical, this means that you cannot record or photocopy any material ideas or tips that are provided in this book.

In this book, we're going to talk about exploring the country of Turkey. So, let's get right to it!

In the United States, when we think of turkey we immediately think of Thanksgiving dinner. However, the word "turkey" is also used for the country of Turkey that connects Europe to Asia.

Where is Turkey?

The country of Turkey is actually a large peninsula. At its northern border is the Black Sea. At its eastern border is the Aegean Sea. At its southern border is the Mediterranean Sea. Turkey has a larger amount of landmass than the state of Texas.

ISTANBUL is its largest city. It is located on a piece of land that is in the Bosporus Strait, which forms a boundary between the continent of Europe and the continent of Asia.

What are the geographic and natural features of Turkey?

The country of Turkey lies on the North Anatolian fault line, which stretches for hundreds of miles from the Marmara Sea located in the west to the Anatolian Highlands in the east. There have been 13 large earthquakes there within the last seven decades. In fact, the fault is so active that it moves about 8 inches annually.

Cracked road after earthquake

Mount Ararat is the tallest mountain in the country. It has two peaks and its tallest peak, called Great Ararat, is a height of almost 17,000 feet. Many people think the mountain is sacred. One of the reasons is because it's where Noah's Ark is thought to have remained after the Great Flood that is discussed in the Bible.

One of the amazing geological features of Turkey is the Pamukkale white cliffs. They are located in western Turkey and they are made of travertine, a mineral that is rich in calcium. From a distance, these cliffs look as if they have a sheet of ice over them. There is a cascade of water that is 1.7 miles long as the spring flows from one pool to another.

Turkey's location as a bridge between two continents is important to people and it's also important to migratory birds. It's on their path from the summer to their winter homes. They congregate at Kus Golu, also called Bird Lake. The lake is in a protected forest and because it's shallow it's the ideal habit for many different species of birds. There are over 250 different species that have been seen there including blue herons and pygmy cormorants.

Just as Turkey's history has been affected by the two continents it bridges, the same is true of its plant and animal life. Some of the plants and animals that have been found there are typical of the Mediterranean countries and other flora and fauna are related to Middle Eastern wildlife.

Sand daffodil, Turkey's endemic plant.

There are two major types of terrain in Turkey. The central as well as the southeastern sections of the country are too arid for trees to thrive there. Instead, those regions are mostly covered in grasslands. The rest of the country used to be primarily forests. However, people have made Turkey their home for so long that most of these natural areas have been changed to pastures or farms.

What is the Culture Like in Turkey?

Because the country of Turkey was conquered so many times, its population is quite diverse. Most people live in the urban areas and children who want to get a high school education must live in the city. Most of the population is Sunni Muslim, an orthodox form of Islam. About 20% of the population is Kurdish. The Kurdish people have been trying to establish their own country for a long time. Many Turkish meals consist of

TURKISH DELIGHT WITH ROSE LEAVES

lamb with yogurt sauces and eggplant. Kebabs made with grilled lamb are a favorite dish. For dessert, there is Turkish delight, which is a type of candy that is sometimes flavored with rose petals.

Like the Brazilians, the Turkish people are crazy about soccer and there are three well-known soccer teams based in the city of Istanbul. They are also very competitive with weightlifting as well as Turkish wrestling.

TURKISH TRADITIONAL WRESTLING

What is the history of Turkey?

The settlement of Catal Hoyuk was one of the earliest places where people had dwellings. It was built over 8,800 years ago and is a maze of 150 homes that are joined together. The homes were constructed from mud and since there are no streets, the people who lived there had to get in by climbing into their roofs! The central region of Turkey was once called Anatolia.

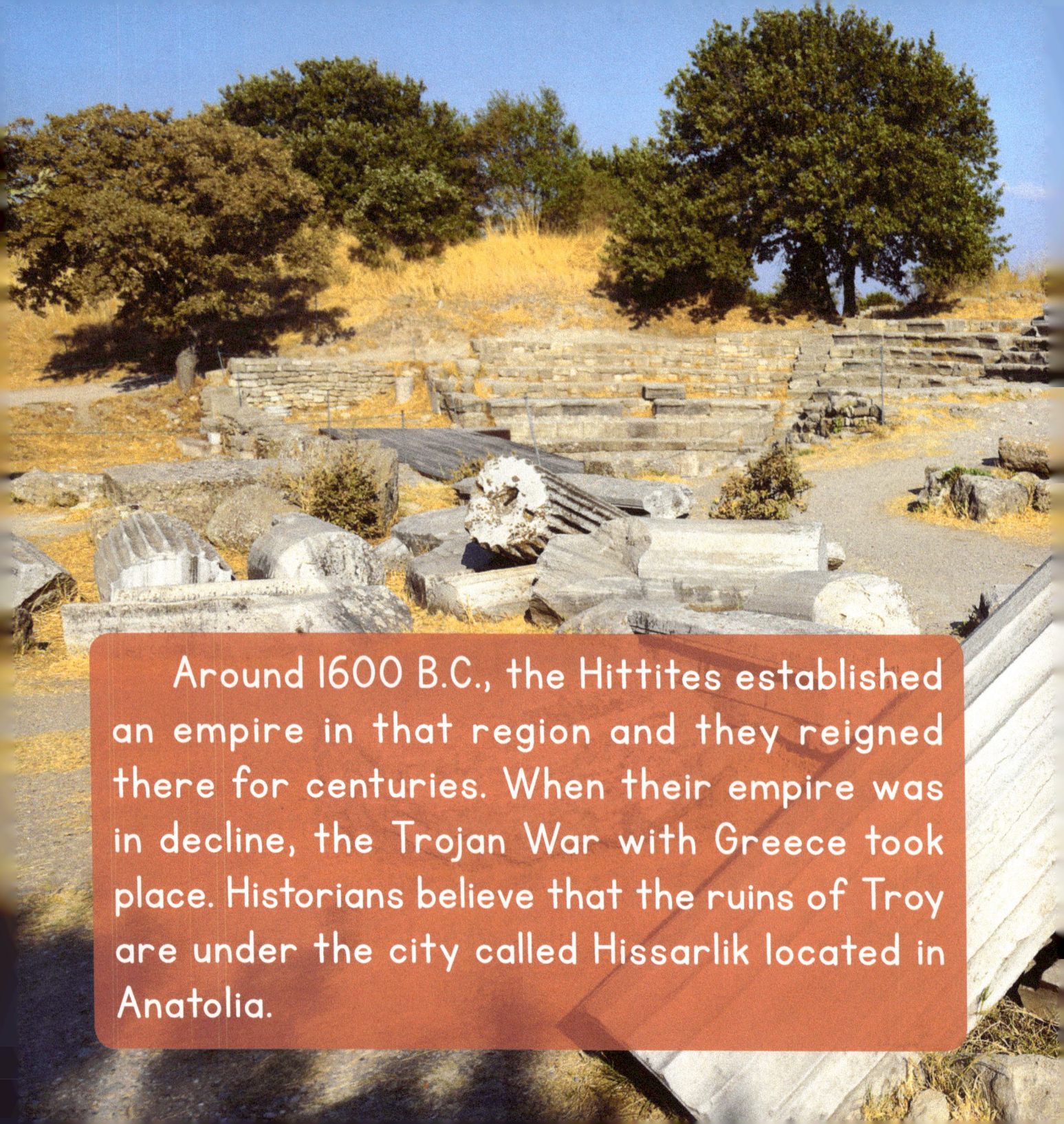

Around 1600 B.C., the Hittites established an empire in that region and they reigned there for centuries. When their empire was in decline, the Trojan War with Greece took place. Historians believe that the ruins of Troy are under the city called Hissarlik located in Anatolia.

Ancient ruins in Troy Turkey

STATUE OF ALEXANDER THE GREAT

The legendary King Midas was the ruler of west Turkey about 700 B.C. The famous conqueror Alexander the Great was victorious over Anatolia in 334 B.C. and brought it under Greek rule. The Roman Empire eventually carved out Anatolia for itself and it became part of the Roman section of Asia Minor.

The Roman Emperor, Constantine, created a new capital there in 330 A.D. named after himself—Constantinople. After Rome fell, it came under the rule of the Byzantine Empire.

The Ottomans invaded the country in 1453 A.D. and conquered Constantinople. Turkey was then a portion of the land that was ruled by the Ottoman Empire. Greece invaded the country after the First World War, but Turkey fought for its own independence, which it won in 1923 when the city's name was changed from Constantinople to Istanbul. At that point in time, Turkey became a country where there was a separation between government and religion.

After the Second World War, Turkey was one of the United Nation's founders. It is also a member of NATO, the North Atlantic Treaty Organization.

FLAGS OF THE MEMBER STATES OF THE NORTH ATLANTIC TREATY ORGANIZATION (NATO)

Interior of the Hagia Sophia in Istanbul, Turkey

What places are good for exploring in Turkey?

There are many beautiful places to explore in Turkey. Here are a few places that you may want to visit.

Aya Sofya

Would you like to see one of the most beautiful buildings in the world? Then, you will want to visit the Aya Sofya Museum.

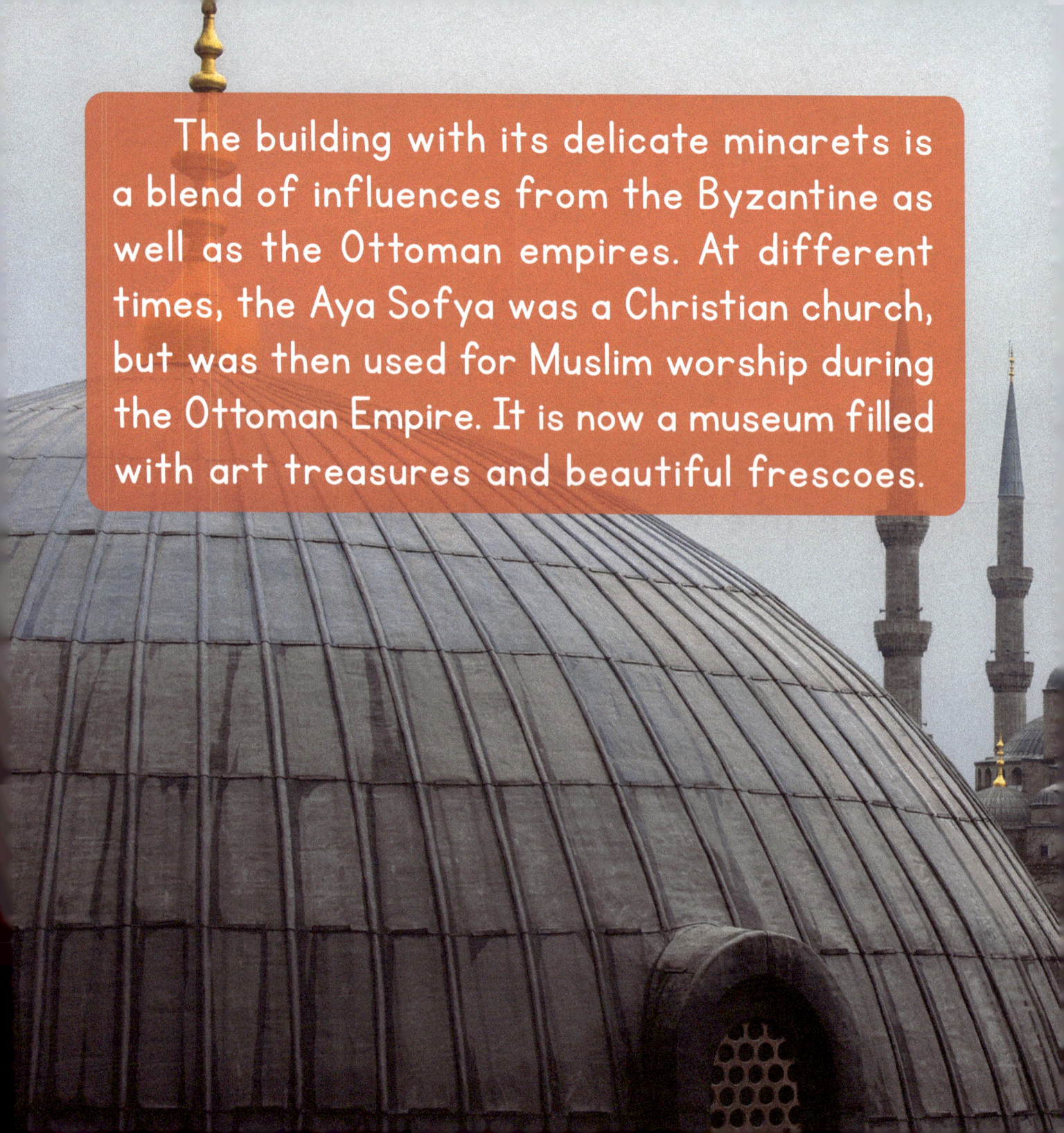

The building with its delicate minarets is a blend of influences from the Byzantine as well as the Ottoman empires. At different times, the Aya Sofya was a Christian church, but was then used for Muslim worship during the Ottoman Empire. It is now a museum filled with art treasures and beautiful frescoes.

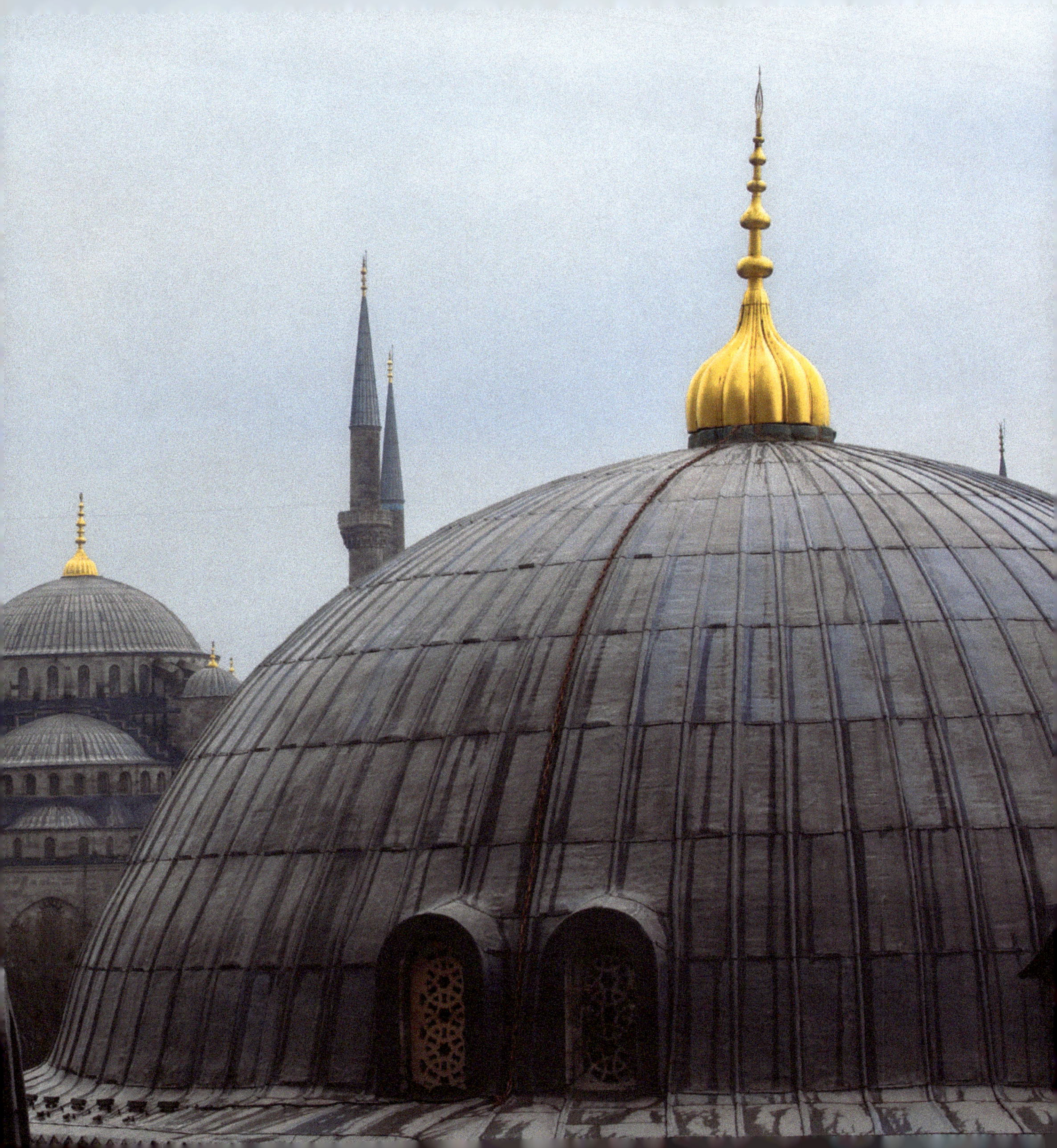

HOT AIR BALLOON FLYING OVER SPECTACULAR CAPPADOCIA

CAPPADOCIA

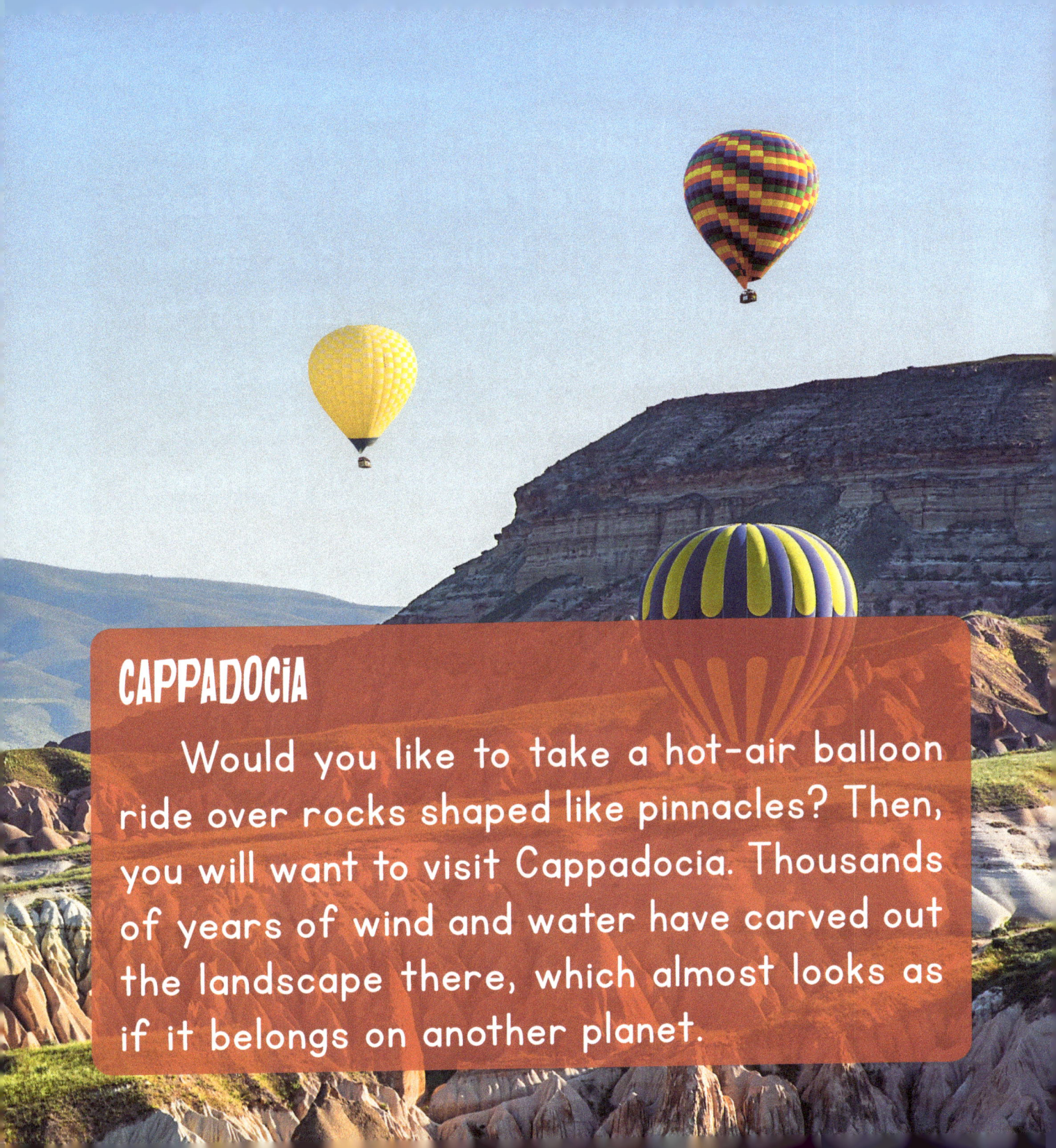

Would you like to take a hot-air balloon ride over rocks shaped like pinnacles? Then, you will want to visit Cappadocia. Thousands of years of wind and water have carved out the landscape there, which almost looks as if it belongs on another planet.

People go hiking to look at the wave-shaped and pinnacle rocks. Some visitors like to take hot-air balloon rides above the unusual landscape. In addition to the interesting geological formations, there are also many Byzantine churches composed of rock with beautiful frescoes on their walls.

RUINS OF A BYZANTINE CHURCH

Entrance of the Topkapi Palace, Istanbul.

TOPKAPI PALACE

Are you interested in the history of the Ottoman Empire? Then, you will want to visit the Topkapi Palace where the wealthy sultans and their wives lived. At one time the Ottomans reigned over a huge empire that extended from Europe to the Middle East and into Africa.

This palace was where the sultans ruled and it is filled with spectacular tiles and decorations made with jewels. During the 400-year reign of the palace, each sultan constructed additional rooms to suit his wishes.

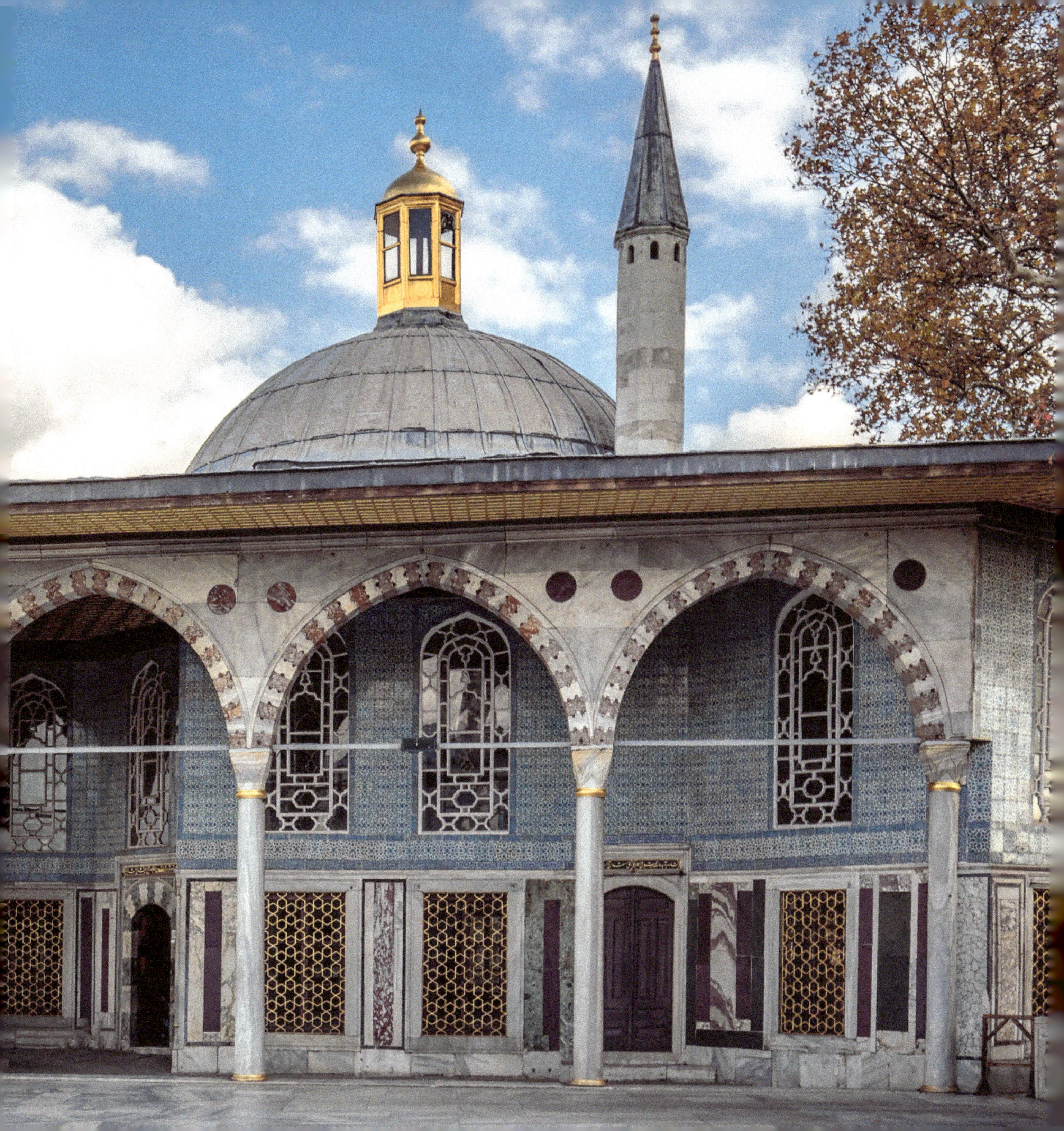

COURTYARD (İFTARİYE KEMERİYESİ) TOPKAPI PALACE

The palace is so enormous that during festival times over 10,000 people stayed there. The Royal Court also had gardens built around the palace that are open to the public today.

PAMUKKALE

Would you like to see one of the world's most amazing natural wonders? Then, you'll want to visit Pamukkale, known as Cotton Castle in English. These amazing cliffs made of travertine hold pools of water that cascade one to the other.

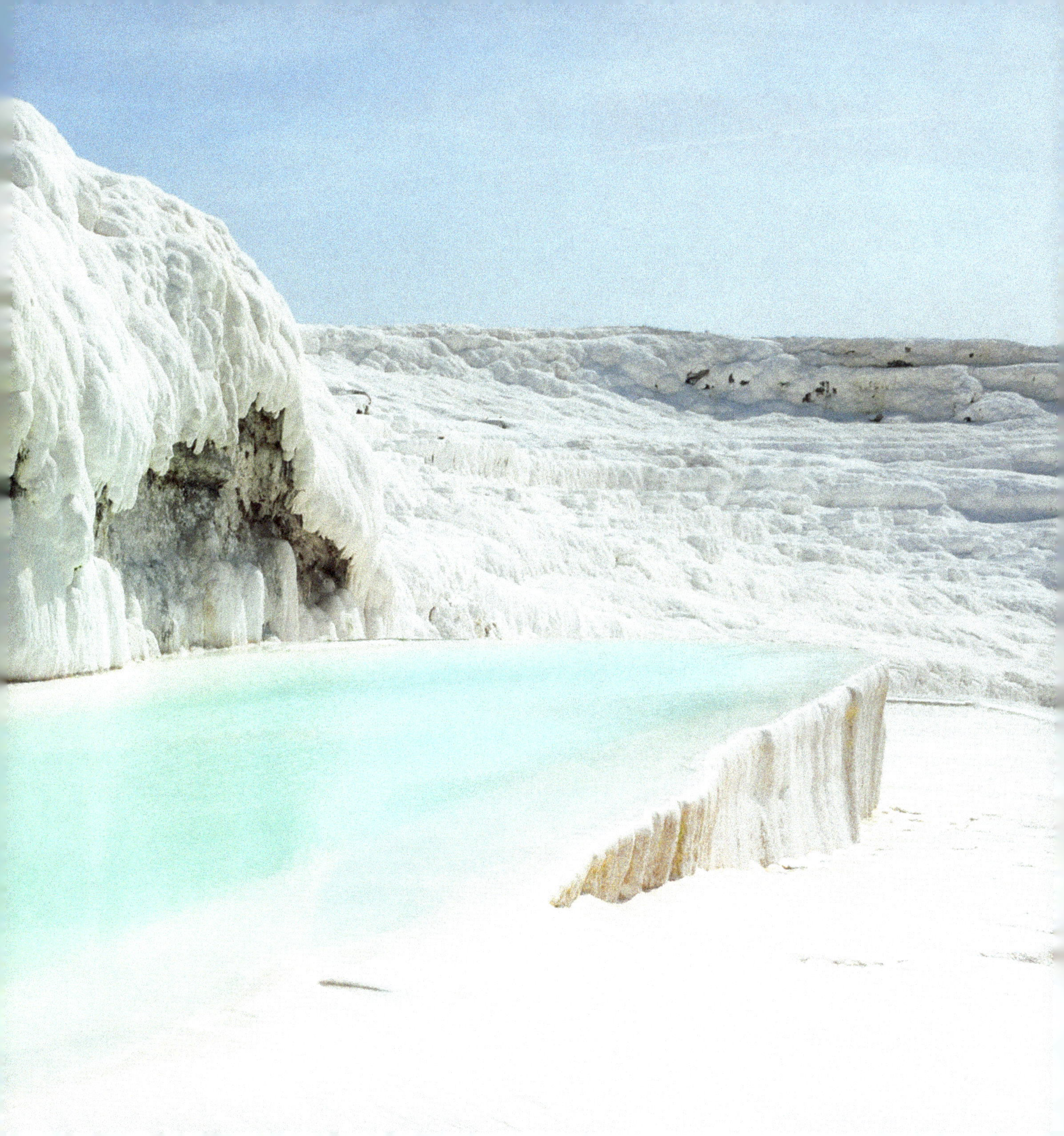

Landscape of Pamukkale

The calcium from the cliffs makes it look like they are made of snow among the landscape of green hills. The surfaces of the cliffs glow as the sun goes down. On top of the hill of calcite is an ancient Roman spa city called Hierapolis.

WHAT HAVE WE LEARNED?

Turkey's location is important because it connects Asia to Europe. It's also important politically since it is located in the Middle East. It is surrounded by three large bodies of water—the Mediterrean Sea, the Aegean Sea, and the Black Sea. Because of its geographic location astride the Anatolian fault line, the country is prone to earthquakes. Turkey has been conquered by many different nations throughout its history, so its population is very diverse. There are many amazing places to see in Turkey from the vistas at Pamukkale to the architectural wonders of Istanbul.

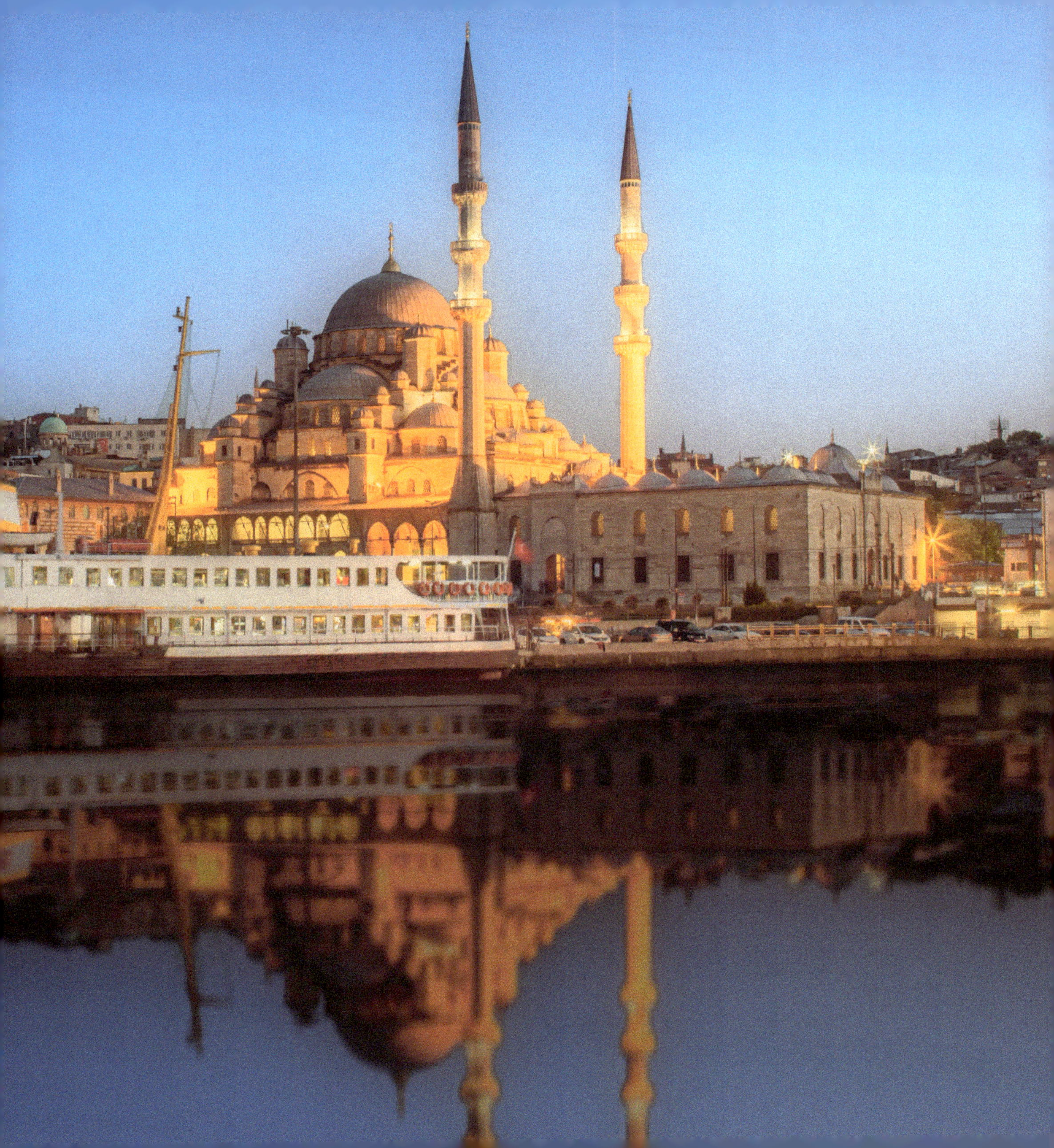

= TU

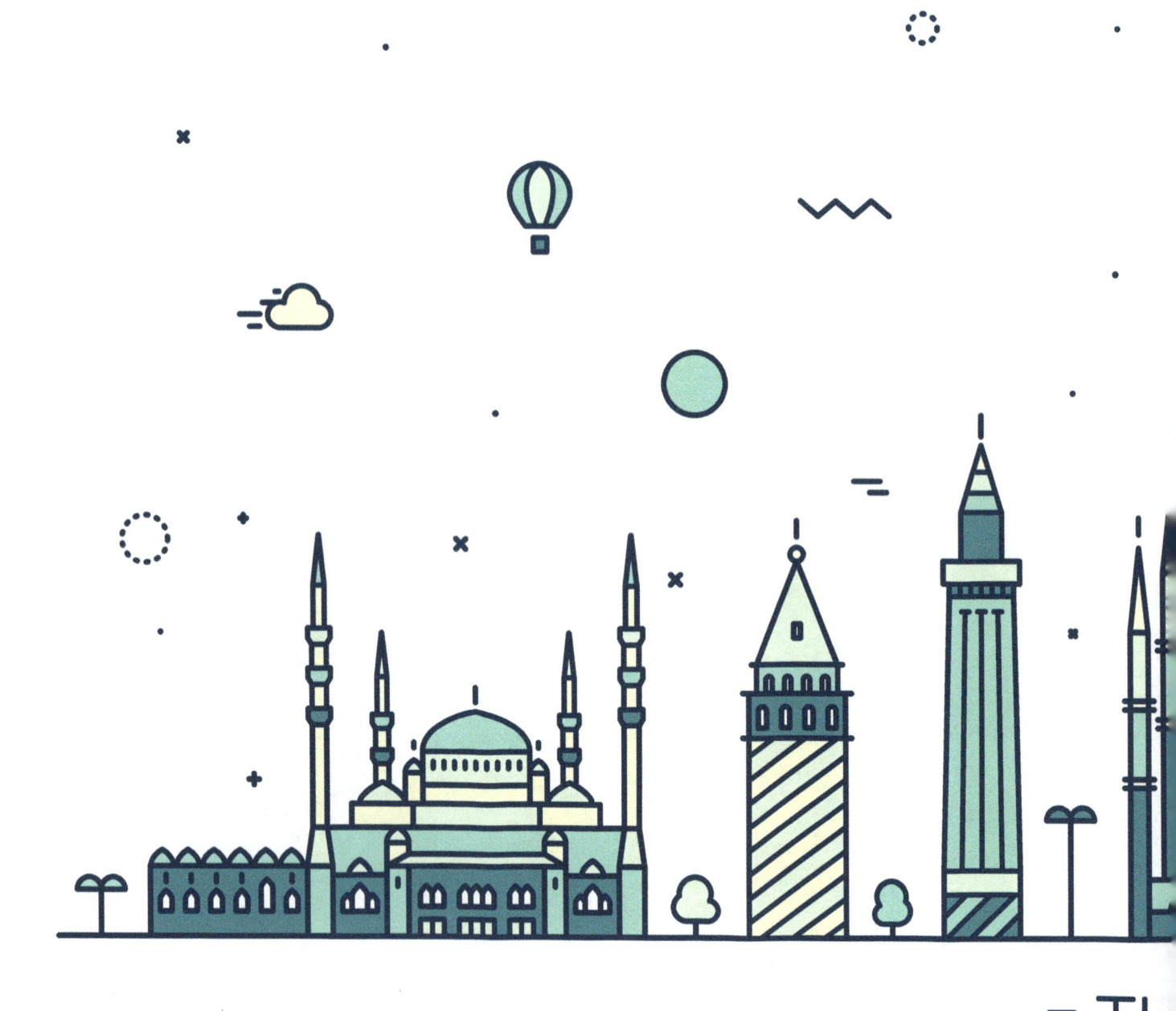

Awesome! Now that you've gone exploring in Turkey, you may want to visit the country of Germany in the Baby Professor book *Is It Germany or Deutschland? Geography 4th grade.*

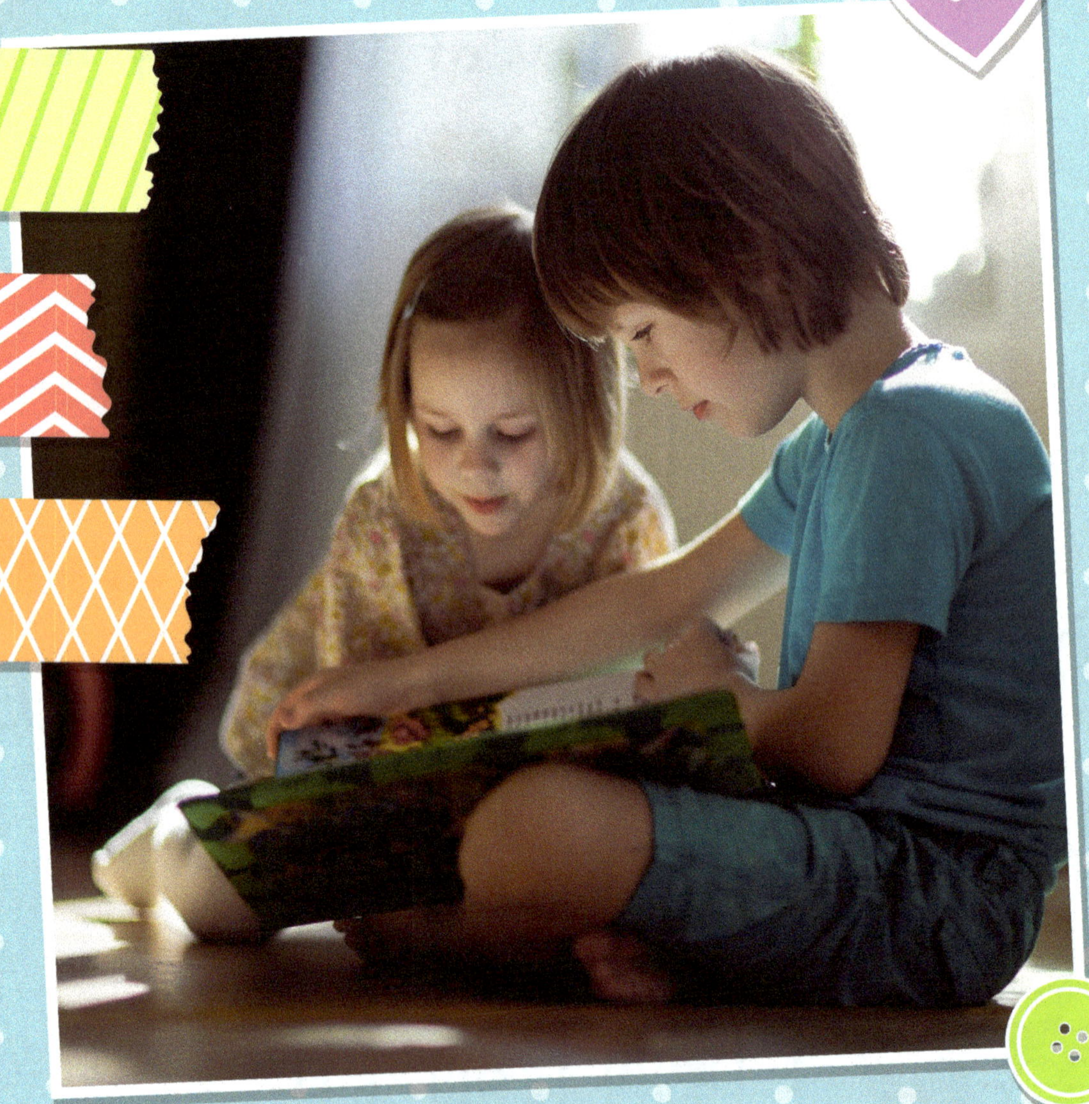

Visit

BABY PROFESSOR
EDUCATION KIDS

www.BabyProfessorBooks.com

to download Free Baby Professor eBooks
and view our catalog of new and exciting
Children's Books

Milton Keynes UK
Ingram Content Group UK Ltd.
UKHW021311160724
445750UK00037B/804

9 781541 915855